For my brother David

May the fire never die in you

Return

Empty Cathedrals

Empty cathedrals
The stone walls of my heart- echoing
The footfalls of glory departing
The ceaseless dripping of complaint
Has stalactites forming in my inner parts. Heaving
To maintain appearances. Makeup on the
Corpse of my life. Empty
Until silent fire appears in the temple
The face of Jesus as he reaches for my
Trembling hands and invites me to walk
Through green gardens. My heart
Is an empty pot rushing over its
Limits with the unhindered love
The unpetitioned
Love. The unrequited but unshakable
Love of Jesus for me
I am lost to all other things
The noise of this world becomes the background
Advertisements and his voice is the
Text notification of a message from my lover
My heart hears his knock and jumps
To reach the door in time. Oh Jesus,
Never leave me.

He steals in the unguarded
Backdoor of your theology and
Washes away the dry, stale bread
Image of God. Knocking down the statues

We are the fire tenders
We welcome the broken in from the cold
To the warmth and the light of love
The only thing strong enough
To keep the monsters at bay
To scare off our demons
The logs of this fire are
An undying loyalty to Jesus
The willingness to follow him to hell
And a sacrificial love that does not shrink
From cleaning up feces
I will not let the steely glint fade from my eyes
As I fix my entire life's path on one goal
To trod unswervingly towards his face
To know him more than I know any other thing
To fear nothing in my path
To be holy as he is holy
And to tend the fire even when I am old
Have arthritis in my hands and
Cataracts in my eyes
Though I go blind
I will not leave this path

All these things sit on my chest
Unsaid
Like a ten story building
They push me into the ground. I am
Ground into powder, left muted
Mute.
.

And the pathway to truth lies
Before me. A winding road that leads
Through a valley of thorns to a gate
Few will enter. Why can't I speak?
Force out a sound. I am tethered in nets
And pulled to the depths. I scream
In my mind but nothing comes out. Oh
Tender you, can you not
Enter my head, see all the truth inside and
Pull it out of me without a sound? I cannot
Speak. My tongue clings to the roof of my
Mouth. I can count all my
Bones. And I cannot speak
Oh Spirit, help me in my weakness
I do not know what to pray. Come
Cry out for me with wordless groans
The silent poetry of anguished spirit
I throw myself on love with no other
Way of escape.

My love is like streams
It falls to the easiest path
It changes its mind
I am inner commotion
I am lack of direction
I rush with passion
Then cool in wide places
But your love is like fields
My heart grazes in green places
I never find the edges
You invite me to rest
I am whole again

I Am

Pioneer

I am seeking deeper
I haven't found the edges of you
You live in children's eyes
You break out the cracks near
The edges of ancient faces
You swirl in the colors of fresh fruit
You soar in the eastern window.
Riding dawn's momentum
You are dance and mystery
I feel you in leper colonies
I chase the hints of glory
The wisps of what is good
And deeply true
My feet are on the path
That climbs your mountain
And any other thing has lost
Appeal. Joy fights gravity
Hurls me god-ward
I am happily lost on the road
To your home

Spoke
And the universe stood still
The ancient words
The scars written beforehand
On our hearts
The internal bleeding
The name of our healing
What a radical soothe
What a political pacifist
Revolutionary
Anarchist
Poet yet realist
Poor yet healer
Lie breaker
Puzzle speaker
Lover of the least
Hater of the hypocrite
Lord of the feast
The Son who inherits all
And rises with strength
To beat down injustice
Mountain hiking vagabond
Traveling bard
Friend of the wind
Holder of mystery
Enigmatic socialist
New wine
Holy dirt
Son of man
Truest friend

Hinges slowly creaking
Oak swinging on iron
Pins. Color spills inside
Outside tumbles in
Yesterday wheezes and slips
Out a defeated breath
Life is sun that soaks all
Life is music that tears through
Walls. Life is the kiss that wakens
Love. Waking all to awe and
The art of losing excuses. Loosing
The knotted tendencies restricting
Our youth, degenerating our dreams
Ripping the seams of our wonder
Leaving us under the spell of decay
Life is the creeping in of day
The replacement of nay saying
With fearless yessing
Wind steals softly
Lifting sails proudly
Wild hearts blazing
Pushing us to open sea

Let love be in me
And let it be so
Strong that it sears my throat
And chokes up in my mouth
Competing for air. That I would not
Eat if I have not loved. That my
Ribs would burn white hot
With it. That it would melt through
This shell of death and paint me
In colors of heaven. That I would
Smell like love and look
Like love looks in every situation
That I would dress like love
Because I put on Christ
That my neurons would be invaded
By true love that swallows
Even the last throes of hatred in me
Let love be all until I
Am swallowed in love and known
By no other name than
Love

I am all frail things
A weak heap of twigs and
   Longings.
  You hover like a
    Mother and sing songs to me

Build up the walls of my heart
     They are caving in
Breath iron and fire into me

   The melody I used to know

   I am emptiness and deserts
 And too blind to even remember
    Home.
      Or my name
       Or the shape
        Of your face
   (Make me strong)

Zeal

Wildman
Knife in hand
Son spared for a lamb
Last minute substitution
Rejection of death
Rugged warrior
Soul in hand
Sons bought with blood

No one takes this life from me
I give it

Acceptance of death
Surrendered so we could be saved
Wildman
Digging up graves
Mocking death
Honoring the slain
He rises like victory
And all darkness flees
Yes even the sky rolls up
Like a scroll
And my sins shrivel and wither
In the glorious light
Of the loveglow of his face
The waterfall of his voice
The tenderness of his presence
Wildman
Tearing up my heart
Making it a new building
Dangerous and good remodeler
Restoring the paths to the father

Freedom flows like a
Virus through my veins
I have been infected with the truth
And I cannot shut down
Cannot shut out these
Voices in my head that sing
The choral arrangements
Of refusing to die
Or giving up in the face of tyranny

I will not betray my kin
I will rise from ashes and always
Join the martyrs who stand as pillars

Fiery poles in the fence that divides
The corrosive oppression
I am the sword of fire
Slavery will forever be banished
From the land of the free

The kingdom of the lowly

Don't shut down

Don't give up

Don't stop breathing

Painting
Seething
Feeling

I will breath every star into
My lungs and scream the quiet
Roar they sing through me

The strength of the universe
The joy of unveiling the mystery
Musk and rain and fiery leaves
Burning bushes at Walden's pond

      Stir me and lure me to the wild things
      The uncaged things
      The things with no names or price tags
      Or cares. I am barefoot here

And my naked toes conduct the
Electricity of all things
As if I am the lightning rod
And they have all chosen me

To be the confused and wandering pilgrim
Scrambling for the words to describe this hunger in me.
To try to decide if I should cry
Or sing at the deep
And cutting sadness
In the face of beauty

The dying sun rips tears from me
      Of joy or grief I can't tell
      So I call them stars and let them
            Fall back into the ocean

         With all their brothers

         The tears of the saints

    The woken children who still love

    The earth and have learned to

    Hear its song

      With both lungs I sing along

You

The only reason

From the start. How my heart

Creaks and aches on the inside

How it wrestles and moans

To return to these foggy fields

To taste first love again

To hear your voice in wind

Life finally realizing meaning

Wandering

And then stumbling

Out of the trees at the peak

Clarity is beautiful

How I have missed you

Waking up is not just opening eyes
        Waking up is keeping eyes closed
        And only letting real things
        Seep through pores
        Drinking wind and cold and
                Morning. Knowing birds through
                Song. Waking is rousing
                Not just body but heart
                It is hurling headlong into
                        Freezing lakes in hopes that
                        Adrenaline and a desperation for
                        Survival will keep you from lazily
                        Letting beauty pass by the
                                Half-sleeping eyes of your soul

When breezes are still
And fog disappears
And the mountains find their twins
In the glass of the lake
                    When motors die and are buried
                        In berry patches outlasting
                        Even the last echo of man's
                    Confusion- his great progression
                                And advancement
When the birds return
        Because all is safe
            And the deer steal silently
                    Back into the open

Then my soul will also shed its worries
Packed like unneeded things
In a canvas knapsack
I will leave it by the water's edge
For the tide to consume
As I glide like the moon
Up the grassy hills into skyland
Untethered and spilling wildly
        Like the rivers to the sea
                Finally free

We follow nail-scarred hands
That invite us to die
We do not live on photo shoots
Or accolades. Our destiny is the glory
Of being forgotten, downtrodden
And rotten in jail cells
Names defamed and written like curses
Graffiti on the subway walls
A cry in the night that can never be silenced
That will wake the dead and the sleeping
We will sow our lives as the last battle cry
Passing the baton to another generation
Revolution will never die
They could never silence truth with lies
I resist violence and refuse to
Become a part of the machine by joining
The employment of violent means
Peace kills all war
Suffering engulfs the violence and ends
Every cycle of revenge
I take the arrow to the heart
And extinguish it forever
Love calls out through storms
And embraces its own killer

It is the final fight

He is more lovely to me
Than anything my soul could think of

Yes, this muscle, my heart
Was only made to be focused on him
I am a misused instrument
Living at the cinema
Misdiagnosing all my diseases
Taping up my symptoms with the
Placebos of part time relationships
With broken people

                        'Come' he says
                   'and I will give you rest
                 From all your circles. From your
                     Shortness of breath. Let me
                  Breathe real air into your lungs
                  Your sails, so downfallen with the
                 Nothingness of this cotton candy world'
Jesus I come
Not with long titles or fancy sounding names
Not with anything in my past that I am proud of
I come with no money or talents for your kingdom
Bankrupt and shipwrecked
Failed and found wanting
A hungry urchin orphan wandering
The streets alone looking for just

        A morsel of your love

I have looked everywhere but here
I have sought everyone but you
And now I am coming back to the same home
Knocking on the same door
Wanting just a taste of grace
              Now you open the door and take me
                    In to set me by the fire
               To really see me. Looking into my eyes
               You tell me I'm your child and I'll never
                    Be alone. I can not outrun this love
And I am overwhelmed in sloppy
Thankfulness. Jesus, you are the most
Lovely thing my soul can think of

Forwardly expecting the things
I've never known. A sick suspicion
That this life is only shadows
I am the immigrant child studying my
Bloodline in the veins of leaves
Waking as if from an eighty-year
Dream. I toss and mutter in my
Sleep of home
The gold breaking in the clouds
My soul finally un-shrouded

Morning fire rising
Early stretch
        run
             flail
Fall

pitch, dirt, bark
    Knuckles bleeding
    Sweat stained
    Hard breathing

I am at war with giants

Addicted to impossible things

Rising predawn to kill the early worm

And the bird with one stone

Grown from the riverbed of winter's rain

Thawed from the tundra of hardship

Hibernation is over

It's time to sing fire through my eyes

And speak louder than these storms

To let go of my insecurities

And grab the only Rope that's ever held me

I can't hold onto both

When the breezes calm
And all I see is you
Your eyes burn a fire
                    A growing fire

A wildfire that rips through the drying
Brush of my sad and fading obsessions
All these things I sunk my money into
All the trinkets I valued more than the
Happiness of those around me

And I am caught by fire

Burned alive in it

All my things and every
Distinguishing mark are charred by
Love so holy it will not spare
Anything that hinders
I am made free

Our God is a burning fire
And his flame burns like jealousy
Down to the deepest
                    cracks
                        of the heart

Your love is like the morning
Greeting me. Keeping me
From my emptiness
From my days in bed

You are invitations and calls
To recklessness. You are
Joyful determination
You are the anger of a friend

The freezing shower and the
Warm coffee. You restart me
And fill me with good things
With songs and breeze and stars
And purpose and heart

When I am with you I smell
Like pine trees and upward thinking
I forget this world's rhythm
And dance forgetfully along the

Sandy coast. Your love is
Pillars of clouds out at sea
They overwhelm me and I
Forget myself entirely

Storms in me
Clouds and darkness
Rush with wind and power
And keep my heart from seeing
Clearly. I am tossed about
Like a ship at sea
Wanting the stillness
Peace

Words left unsaid
Thoughts left in my head
Dreams abandoned in schematic
Stages. Mockups and vain imaginations
Failing to give birth to reality
I don't want to live on the
Cutting room floor. In constant
Planning meetings with myself
I want to be
To do
To live and breathe
To try and fail
Inhale exhale

Bleed and seethe and fight and dream
And not go quietly into that dark night
But erupt in all the colors I was made of
Before my skin knew air
To use the last drops of this
Short, short life
To sing and be sung
To paint and be painted
To live and be life
And not just to wish
Not just to hope without wings

Oh raging river
Oh frigid brink of death
Come wake me
Turn me from my apathy
Scrape the skin from my knuckles
Fill my belly with songs and fire
Steel me in the forge
Shake me from hibernation

A Psalm For the Longing Heart

Is it better to be destroyed
In this great yearning?
To be confused and unsatisfied
All my life? Never reaching
The top or the end?

                    Or would it be better
            Having this world's treasure
                  To be fooled into rest
                To be happy and content
            With these passing shadows
                  With rust and dust?

        I remain happily anguished
        Let me never fall asleep

My head is filled with stew
The strange soup brewed from
My sick aching for home
The boiling in my bones

A longing. This strange weight
On my chest leaving me unsatisfied
With every fleeting wonder
It all escapes me like ash on the rising

Smoke. It flies into stars on Orion's Belt
So ancient yet consistently distant
Never attainable. And would it be better

To spit out the last drops of this
Water I have tasted? To punish my tongue
For ever knowing that joy unreachable

Should I wipe my mind of the memories
The hints of that otherness I drank
On the ridge lines of the continental divide
Flirting with fog, spattered with pines?

Should I teach myself to be fine
With the morning paper, polarized politics
And a self gutted of wonder?

I still don't know. Oh, how it hurts
To not be with you, the wind
Freely speeding through valleys
Westward to home

Love
That great messy wind
Blowing at night
Scattering my table
Destroying all my plans
How dangerous and majestic
How mysterious and deeply kind
Are the terrors of his grace
I am dashed on the rocks
And washed up on the shores of him
I've never been happier to be ruined
(if anyone is not willing
To give up all and follow me
He cannot be
My disciple)

I struggle with every last ounce of the cry in me
Fighting the slowly advancing wall of
Dark and silent apathy. Trying to drown out the
Revolution that was stitched into my blood. I taste it
Every time I bleed. And every time I breathe
Heavy as I run mountains
And every time the gleam of morning rises
And reminds me that all the filthy shadows
Are erased in the light of his face
Jesus is my new day
He is winning the war in me
My sustenance and victory.

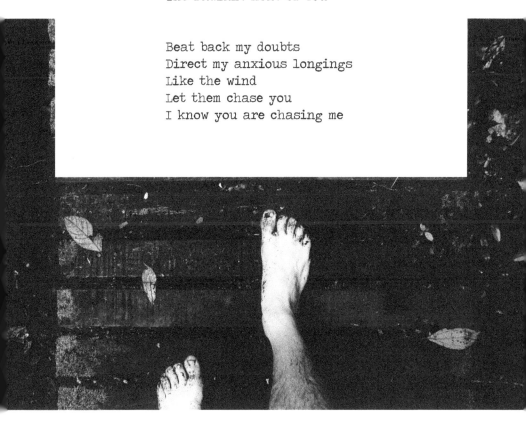

Morning is gold and turquoise
Fire rising silently
Love grows slow in the form of day
Before my clouds obscure
The radiant heat of You

Beat back my doubts
Direct my anxious longings
Like the wind
Let them chase you
I know you are chasing me

Breathe the firesong of morning

Taste the firstfruits of glory

For the times when I'm weak

I will pull out the songs of fire
I will dust off the war photographs of my grandfather
And think of the way he stared down fear
Because no one else would. When I am
Weak. I will think of three young men
Who would not kneel to the golden
Statue system of this age. The gutter punks who
Followed the Son of Man into flames. I will think
Of Peter crucified upsidedown and wonder
What kind of love could have filled his heart
That he was more addicted to Jesus than to air
And wonder if that love could infect me too
If it could keep me from being this American zombie
Consumer, sleeper, Netflix binger
Shutter of eyes and of heart
For the times when I am too weak to be a warrior
But too strong to fall helpless onto mercy
I will call out in the dark
For the Spirit of the Warrior to
Haunt the temple of my body
Make me into something God-like
Strong

I have switched off
That small voice
In my brain that speaks
Fear and pain and weakness
The one that loves getting attention
I killed him
And let myself run like rivers
At the speed of gravity
Ripping through bark and gravel
I am lightning in the dark of night
When I rise on Monday
I hear no complaining
About another week starting
I run with the rhythm of machines
And ignore the complaining of my body
Steady and consistent
To earn the money I need
To buy a tank of gas
And drive to a trailhead
I'm an addict
To high places and mountain air
Where my spirit can breathe clean
And my mind can think clearly
And I will unflinchingly bear all things
Just to get there

I'm holding on for dear life
Yes dear
        sweet
            life
That wild forest nectar
Poured daily into our jars
Equally and without discretion
I will patch every hole in my clay
To catch as much as I can
To guard it like a smoldering beach fire
Of driftwood uncovered from sand
And wonder-embers kept eternal

To smear my body with its flame
Like warpaint mashed from
River rocks

Raging wildly like oldworld warriors
Against the slow kind of death
When life leaks from battered pots
Wasted moments spilling
Unappreciated to the ground
Soaking into the thirsty earth
        May we never lose our wonder

You stand
A shadow on the shoreline
A bridge between surf and sand
Wanting, leaving, softly breathing

Speaking to the waves
Orchestrating their every falling

Fish slowly simmering
Mediterranean breakfast

Light trickling from the east
All night I spilled my sweat
        I hauled the ropes and cast the nets
        Spent, aching, muscle exhaustion
        Depleted, defeated, quitting my causes

Giving in and letting my heart
Keel over and sleep in the boat
But one word from the coast

My name

And I feel the blood
        Reaching my brain again
        I feel the winter winds on my skin
        And a courage that swells from my
        Innermost being. Hearing and seeing

My true identity
I rise like a Phoenix
I dive to Atlantis
I swim all the fathoms between us
I finally reach you
My odyssey
My Everything

Rabbi

I am reaching for him
In all my purchasing and talking
And boasting and running and seeking
And knowing and eating and falling
And hurting and running scared into the
Woods. I am reaching for him
Like a child. Like a small, small thing
Powerless and frustrated. Why does
Nothing taste like him? Oh world of
Lies and cotton candy. Can't you see I'm
Trying
Trying
Lying and punching and getting drunk
This is all my broken reaching. Hungering
For what's underneath. Oh naked longing
For the one called Love
Oh bitter disappointment that comes
Running out at every bite of all things
That are not him
Will I only be satisfied in death?
I am trying

In a garden all alone

He comes and gives me better clothes

Than graveclothes. A stone with a new

Name. A house prepared for me

I am not seeking I am sought

I am not searching I am searched

Intensely. A gaze that blazes from a bush

And burns through my eyes into my heart

Seeing all the broken things I hide there

Nowhere to run and I am undone

Frightened by the love I thought I always wanted

Scared at the cost

He stands at the shoreline and demands

That I abandon my job and my friends

I've found him, the one my heart longs for

Yet my knees are too weak to leave

The beggar's mat, these empty nets

Send your spirit like a dove

Make me strong enough to love

I'm trying

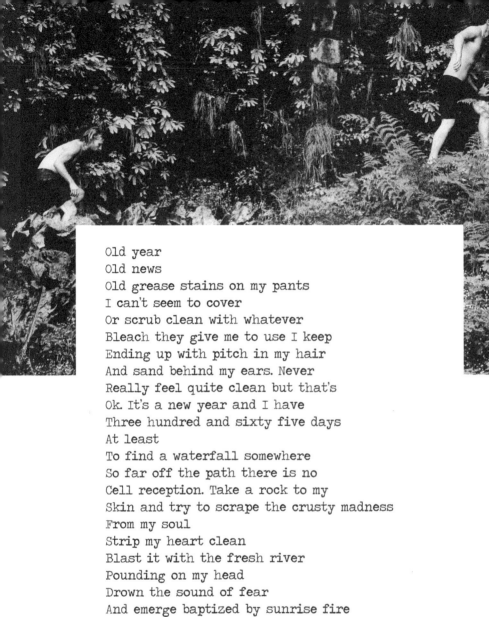

Old year
Old news
Old grease stains on my pants
I can't seem to cover
Or scrub clean with whatever
Bleach they give me to use I keep
Ending up with pitch in my hair
And sand behind my ears. Never
Really feel quite clean but that's
Ok. It's a new year and I have
Three hundred and sixty five days
At least
To find a waterfall somewhere
So far off the path there is no
Cell reception. Take a rock to my
Skin and try to scrape the crusty madness
From my soul
Strip my heart clean
Blast it with the fresh river
Pounding on my head
Drown the sound of fear
And emerge baptized by sunrise fire

Unchained from the ocean floor

Unburdened of all myopic obsession

Untethered from the other ox

The rotting corpse of my old self

The carrion I carried on my back

In love with all my sickness

Now I am

Finally free to think straight

To breathe deeply and without fear

To hold your hand and trust you

Follow rivers to the sea
Follow ants back up the tree
Follow sparks to stars
Thoughts to hearts
Follow beauty back to the start
Before we broke
Before the scars grew in our skin
Before we doubted the words
That spill off our lips
Crashing lifelessly to the ground
Scattered ceramics
Burning maps
Teenage angst
(All I want is to believe you)
Before the barbed wired defenses
Before the gaslamp excuses
Before the knives and the nooses
The loosely firing pistons
The echoing distance

.

Follow the breadcrumbs
The red yarn through the woods
Back to a hidden garden
Where I traded my soul for soup
Past the flaming sword
Follow it home

The desert unfurls pink flowers
Like flags of defiance
Screaming 'I'm not dead
I'm not dead' centuries may pass
Of drought and death
Even so first rain raises the bloom
Of life, the songs from night come
Whistling into arid space
Stripping decay from the
Neverdying Spirit underneath
Caught up in the skies

The Catechism

Where will we dream?
On this handknit rug
By this oak fire on the hearth
With coffee and journal in hand
We will dream

Where will we live?
Not only wrapped in ourselves
But spilling out into the street
Where the broken and hurting live
Where the sinners lose their way
We will live

How will we know God's will?
In much seeking and confusion
In an orchestrated catastrophe
That often looks like a mess
But a mess that brings us closer each moment
To the Father's heart
In tears and longing and much time
Will we know God's will

How can we forgive?
By fixing our eyes on the one who died
So that we could learn to do the same
By taking the axe to our self-seeking desires
And leaving the bloody stumps writhing in freedom
By learning to forget
We can forgive

When will you trust me?
When I take every last layer of clothing off my heart
And you see my soul stark naked
When you know me as I truly am
And see that all I ever want is Jesus
Will you trust me

What will we tell our children?
That the road was long
With many twists and turns
That we didn't know the answers from the start
And that the journey was always sweeter with Him
Will we tell our children

How will we die?
With much longing in our hearts
Towards the one we were made for
With anticipation and gratefulness
With joy and anticipation
Of all things finally made right
Will we die

Why do you ask?

I am the child of a thousand suns
Not one
Passed me by without open eyes
Without hearty tries and healthy failures
Without waking up and rolling out of bed
Yes
I can gladly shout that all my days
However dreary have been days
That my time, however dragging
Has always rolled on
That my heart, however broken
Has not stopped pumping

And maybe this is the greatest gift
Life itself

The ability and willingness to exist
Even in a broken existence
The privilege of breathing in and out
Of dying once a night
And rising back to life every morning
To join in the song again

To feel pain and cold and joy and family

To rage and writhe and seethe and not give up

And to drink deeply of life

Until the last drop runs out

Arid desert sugar pines

Gourmet coffee music vibes

Tuesday sabbath resting life

Stretching in the morning light

Breathing in the forest wine

Spirit playlist waking soul

Ted talks artist inspiration

Innovation aching for the

Aesthetic of the kingdom

The newness of unborn

Freedom. Paint spilled

Without regret on the canvas

Gravity controlling the madness

Morning devotion to artistic greatness

The crowds tore at him
Voraciously hungering for him
And he spread
        Like bread

And fed five thousand people in an hour
And they took him up in baskets
Yes they gathered his remains in baskets
And placed it in a cave
And the women wept for they could not
Pour oil and spice upon him

   This is the bread that comes down

   From heaven. This is the bread who

   Does the will of his father

      All who eat of him will never die
                    Lonely

Thrive

Not just survive

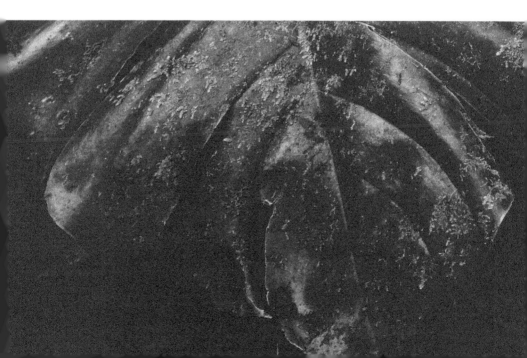

I remember the way

I remember the way to your house

It is a small cobblestoned road

That leads past the crack dens

The girls on the corners, selling

Themselves. It winds past cemeteries

And through living rooms

It is a slow road, with many

Conversations along the way

Inviting travelers to ask questions

To see their worth. To join me

On the way to your house

What a shame to show up alone

As so many runners do, boasting

In their speed. Yes, they beat everyone

To the finish line and weep that they

Ran so fast

And when I pray my tongue

Sticks to the roof of my mouth

    And nothing sound

    Comes out. Just the whimper

        Of the whispering spirit

            Whisking for words

            Willing for worth

Come speak something in me

Make sense of all these

    Raging hunger moans for

        The banquet of God

I am thirsty and I do not know

        The way out of the desert

Can it be that I

A moon

Have very little gravity of my own
And that it is you
Drawing me?

        Can it be?

He's coming for you

And all heaven will not be slowed
By feeble walls

The sick construct of our minds

Theories and habits and poisons and excuses
Disintegrate. Grains of sand melting in
Water rushing fast past the glass walls
We thought would keep out the looting God
He is not a *gentleman* knocking at the door of your heart
He is a mad lover
        who will not be deterred and He has
                promised
He will never take no for an answer
                Until
                You finally die
                Of the cancerous 'no' you have chosen

Even then his mercy will be hard to escape

Woe to pious preachers, the teachers of sickness
        The holy gate-keepers who paint my God
                                As the wicked king
                When He gave everything
                And was born as a
                        Middle eastern refugee
                Friend of sinners
                    Bartender
                Night crawler
My Jesus
Hooker-loving,
        Streetfighting
                Fearless
                Hound of heaven.

                What more can he say to you?

Stop listening to untruth.
The airhead gospel of external behavior modification.
        The gutted
                Candy religion of a passionless distant
                        Grandfather God who only wants to
                Slap your wrists and tend to more important
        Duties of running the far reaches of outer space

        My God has fire in his eyes and your name
        Tattooed on his heart and nothing makes him
        More violently angry than the accuser who
            Whispered into your ear that you were
                    Unworthy and unloved.

            You are worthy and you are loved
                    He is El Roi
                    The God who sees

Perhaps

Love is strong enough

To pick us up and wipe the

Cancer from our shattered jars

To breathe the songs back into

Our belonging hearts and set us

Back on hiking feet

Maybe it is bright enough

To burn the addiction from our brains

To swallow up our pain and fix

All the errors in our equations

Maybe it is making a home

For us that we don't deserve

Maybe it's big enough that it will

Chase us down even the road to

Hell and won't let us go even if

We struggle.

Perhaps love is stronger than we are and

And will defeat us in the end

Grace

Surprising

    Terrible, rule-breaking

        Scandalous rain-in-the-desert

        Grace. Washing my mind

          My insides

        Ridiculous awe- inspiring

          Tempting grace

          Self-contradicting overspilling

          Never-dying grace

        That does not ask questions

        Or check identification

    But lathers gifts and love without

Hindrance or restraint

Grace